GUIDE TO
SOUTH AFRICA

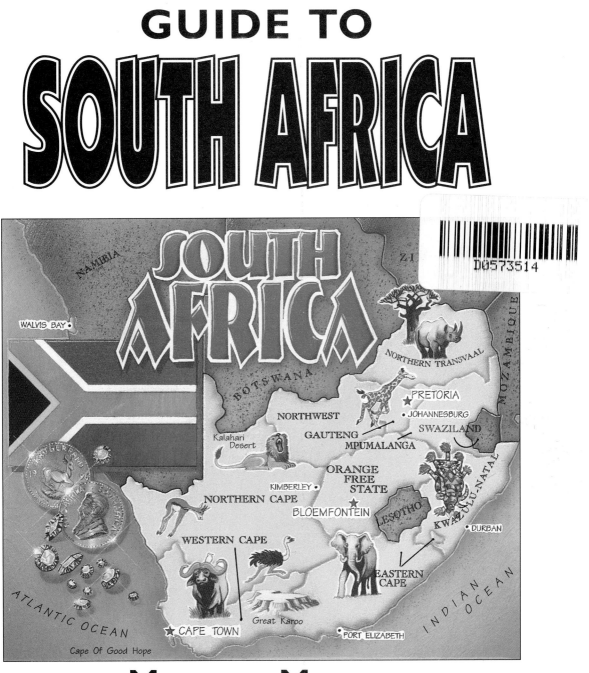

MICHAEL MARCH

Highlights for Children

CONTENTS

On the cover: A street market in Grand
Parade, Cape Town, with City Hall in the
background and Table Mountain in the
distance

Published by Highlights for Children
© 1996 Highlights for Children, Inc.
P.O. Box 18201
Columbus, Ohio 43218-0201

10 9 8 7 6 5 4 3
ISBN 0-87534-930-7

EUROPE

ASIA

AFRICA

AUSTRALIA

South
Africa

ANTARCTICA

△ **The South African flag** The Republic of South Africa chose the six-color flag in 1994 from more than 7,000 designs. The colors are historically the most popular colors for South African flags. Green, gold, and black, for example, are the colors of the African National Congress, South Africa's biggest political party.

SOUTH AFRICA AT A GLANCE

Area 471,442 square miles (1,221,037 square kilometers)

Population 42,741,000

Capital cities Pretoria—administrative (population 1,080,187), Cape Town—legislative (2,350,157), Bloemfontein—judicial (254,780)

Other big cities Johannesburg (1,916,061), Durban (1,137,378)

Highest mountain Champagne Castle, 11,073 feet (3,375 meters)

Longest river Orange, 1,300 miles (2,080 kilometers)

Largest lake Lake Chrissie, 11 square miles (28 square kilometers)

Official languages English, Afrikaans, Zulu, and eight others

▽ **South African postage stamps** Some feature sports. Others highlight the country's art and wildlife.

▷ **South African money** The currency of South Africa is the rand (R). One rand = 100 cents. R100 is the largest note. Wording on bank notes is in both the Afrikaans and English languages.

SOUTH AFRICA

Farmland & Grassland
Desert
Mountains

★ Capital
● Major Cities
▲ Mountain Peaks
— Country Boundary

0 25 50 75 Miles
0 50 100 Kilometers

© Oxford Cartographers

ZIMBABWE

MOZAMBIQUE

Tropic of Capricorn

BOTSWANA

20°S

25°S

Limpopo

Pietersburg

NORTHERN
PROVINCE

NAMIBIA

*Kalahari
Gemsbok
National
Park*

Molopo

★ **Pretoria**

Johannesburg ●

SWAZI-
LAND

Vaal

*Vaal
Dam*

KWAZULU/
NATAL

Vaal

*Bloemhof
Dam*

FREE
STATE

Upington ●

*Champagne
Castle*

Alexander
Bay ●

Orange

Kimberley ●

Bloemfontein ★

LESOTHO

Pietermaritzburg ●

Durban ●

30°S

Orange

CAPE

PROVINCE

Drakensberg

Umtata ●

Great Karroo

East London ●

ATLANTIC

OCEAN

Cape Town ★

*Cape of
Good Hope*

Mosselbaai ●

● Port Elizabeth

INDIAN OCEAN

35°S

N
W — E
S

15°E

20°E

25°E

30°E

5

THE CAPE OF AFRICA

South Africa is a big country at the southern tip of the African continent. It stretches from the Atlantic Ocean on the west to the Indian Ocean on the east. The great Orange River, the longest river in South Africa, forms part of the border with Namibia in the northwest. Another neighbor, the tiny, mountainous country of Lesotho, is completely surrounded by South Africa.

South Africa is famous for its scenery and wildlife. Lions, elephants, hippopotamuses, and other large wild animals can be seen here in their natural surroundings. Along the south coast you can see large colonies of fur seals and seabirds such as cormorants and gannets. Offshore, you might catch a glimpse of whales and dolphins.

The country is mostly warm and dry. But winters in the western part can be cold, with some rain or even snow. However, more rain falls in the eastern part of South Africa, especially during the summer. Here, south of the equator, midwinter comes in July and summer is between November and April.

Most of the country's 42 million people are black. There are many different groups of black people, each with its own traditions, customs, and language. Most of the five million white South Africans are descendants of Dutch and English settlers. The Dutch settlers are called Afrikaners, and the language they speak is Afrikaans. Other people are of mixed or Asian origins.

Religious beliefs are diverse. Many South Africans are Christians, but others follow Islam, Hinduism, and traditional African religions.

▷ **Boats at anchor by Durban's wharf** Durban is a big modern city on the Indian Ocean. It is famous for its surfing beaches.

▽ **The Blue Train winding across rugged countryside** The express train covers the 1,000-mile (1,600-kilometer) journey between Cape Town and Pretoria in just over a day.

▽ **Safari into the bush** A group of tourists watches lions from the safety of a vehicle. Lions are found in major nature reserves all across the eastern part of South Africa.

CITY OF GOLD

South Africa's busiest city is Johannesburg. Nearly two million people—black, white, and others—have their homes here. Their different cultures and customs make this city an exciting place. Anything new in the arts is said to start in Johannesburg.

The city lies in the Witwatersrand hills in the northeastern part of the country. It began as a mining camp just over a hundred years ago and grew rapidly when gold was discovered. Today, Johannesburg's fine old buildings, built with money from gold, stand in the shadow of modern skyscrapers.

You can get a splendid view over the city from the high-rise tower of the Carlton Center. Take the elevator to the revolving viewing platform on the 50th floor. To the north are tree-lined suburbs. To the east, south, and west you can see the sand-colored heaps dug out in gold-mining operations in the Witwatersrand hills.

Shares of gold worth billions of dollars are bought and sold daily on the floor of Johannesburg's Stock Exchange. You can watch the excited dealers at work and take a tour of the historic building.

◁ **A busy street scene in downtown Johannesburg** Some buses have both an upper and a lower deck. Like the British, South Africans drive on the left-hand side of the road.

▷ **Aerial view of downtown Johannesburg** Skyscraper office buildings tower above the long, wide streets of the Central Business District. The checkerboard design of Johannesburg's streets makes it easy for visitors to find their way.

▷ **Colorful market in Johannesburg**
Souvenirs, bags, and African carvings are among the items for sale.

At the Museum Africa you can see an exhibition of an older culture with ancient African rock paintings. There is also a cave built to show how the San people lived. These early African hunters were called *bushmen* by the English settlers.

African masks, souvenirs, and Oriental spices can be bought in the markets. Stores sell everything from clothes to diamonds. You can eat local dishes, such as crocodile's tail or buffalo steak, or choose from a wide range of foreign foods. Traveling around Johannesburg is easy using buses or cabs.

TOWNSHIPS AND MINERS

Johannesburg's fine railroad station is the biggest in Africa. A luxurious train called the Blue Train passes through here on its journey from Pretoria to Cape Town. To be sure of a seat on this special express train, you have to book nearly a year in advance.

The railroad station was built in the 1960s when South Africa was under white rule. The Afrikaner government made laws that forbid black and other nonwhite South Africans to ride in the same coaches as white people. Nonwhites even had to live apart in "townships" built on the edges of the cities. The townships were often poor, with rows and rows of tin shacks for houses.

This way of separating people by race and skin color was called by the Afrikaans name, *apartheid*. Today the laws that enforced apartheid no longer exist, but the townships still do. Every morning thousands of Johannesburg's black workers arrive by train from Soweto, biggest of the townships and home to more than a million people. It lies southwest of the city. The name is a short form of "South Western Township." Protests by the people of Soweto helped bring an end to white rule in South Africa.

Many of the men who work in the gold fields on the Witwatersrand come from Soweto. Black miners have played a big part in gold-mining since it began in the 1880s. Gold Reef City is a living museum that recalls those early mining days. Here, you can put on a miner's coveralls and lamp and go 720 feet (220 meters) down into an old mine to see what life was like underground. You can also watch gold bars being made from the molten metal and be entertained by African dancers wearing feathered head-dresses and floppy rubber boots like those once worn by black miners.

△ **African dishes** *Mealie* (maize), South Africa's main food, is in the bowl on the right. The other plate has tasty fish patties.

▽ **Gold Reef City, Johannesburg** A theme park stands on the site of the old gold mine. Its centerpiece is the rebuilt tower and real mine shaft.

▽ **Smoking chimneys in Soweto** Many of the houses are small and packed close together. Some townships are very poor.

GOVERNMENT AND GAME PARKS

The drive from Johannesburg to Pretoria up the N1 highway takes less than an hour. Pretoria is a city of government buildings and beautiful parks and gardens. In October and November, when the 60,000 jacaranda trees that line the streets come into bloom, Pretoria is a sea of purple.

The city is named after a Voortrekker hero, Andries Pretorius. The Voortrekkers were Boers, or Afrikaners, who left the South African Cape in the 1830s to escape from British rule. They wanted to set up their own states. A huge granite monument to those early pioneers stands on a hill overlooking Pretoria from the southwest.

On a hilltop to the east of the center of the city, you see the red sandstone Union Buildings. These were built as government offices in 1913, after the Boer states became part of a united South Africa. Pretoria is still one of South Africa's three capital cities.

Away from the city, you can visit the Ndebele Show Village. In the village you will see traditional Ndebele huts, painted in bright colors with beautiful patterns. The Ndebele people and the Voortrekkers once fought about land rights.

The biggest and most famous nature reserve in South Africa is Kruger Park. It was started in 1898 by Paul Kruger, the Afrikaner leader. You can fly to the park from Pretoria, or drive through the rocky Drakensberg mountains. Kruger Park's dry grassland (*veld*) and forests are home to lions, leopards, rhinoceros, buffalo, and elephants. Cheetahs, the fastest animals on land, and many other animals and birds also live here. Crocodiles and hippopotamuses share the park's rivers and pools. For a close-up look at some of the "big game" animals, you can follow a hiking trail through the veld led by a park ranger.

▷ **Statue of Paul Kruger, Church Square, Pretoria** Kruger fought against the British. In the 1880s he was president of an independent Afrikaner republic with Pretoria as its capital.

▽ **Church Square in the center of Pretoria** Lovely old public buildings surround the park in Church Square. Today the area around the square serves as a major bus terminal.

▽ **Young Ndebele woman** She wears a beaded headdress and necklace. Beadwork and rug-making are important Ndebele crafts.

ZULU COUNTRY

The Drakensberg mountains are at their most spectacular in KwaZulu-Natal Province. Steep cliffs stretching eastward soar high above the green foothills. Here you will find forests of silvery-pink protea, South Africa's national flower. Here, too, on the border with Lesotho, is Champagne Castle, South Africa's highest mountain. Hikers on their way to the top must be prepared for any weather. A hot sunny day can change to a freezing cold night. Often there are rainstorms and in winter, blizzards.

Pietermaritzburg lies below the Drakensberg foothills. This small historic town was begun by Boer settlers, but was soon taken over by the British. You can visit the Church of the Vow, built by the Boers in memory of their victory over the Zulus at the battle of Blood River.

△ **The huge Jumah Mosque, central Durban** Many of the city's Indian Muslims worship here.

▽ Farming country in Zululand Round huts made of grass, mudbrick, or stone, with thatched roofs, are found all over South Africa.

▽ Ships in Durban's deep-water harbor Durban is one of South Africa's main ports. Huge amounts of goods from abroad arrive here.

The Zulus defeated many other native groups and were a powerful people in the 1820s when they were united under their famous king, Shaka. Today they still have their own king and are the largest nation in South Africa. In country areas many Zulus still live in grass huts, and women wear the traditional fan-shaped headdress.

Hluhluwe game park was once the hunting ground for Zulu kings. Here you will find both white rhino and the smaller, much rarer, black rhino. Female lions, who do most of the hunting for the pride, are often seen on the prowl.

The Indian Ocean lies off the KwaZulu-Natal Coast. Durban is the province's biggest city. Here you can relax on beaches, explore the sea, or surf the waves. Many people have come here from India to work in the sugarcane fields. Today, Durban has more than a million Indians.

THE WILD COAST

The coast road from Durban disappears south of the Untamvuna River. This is the start of 185 miles (300 kilometers) of rocky shoreline called The Wild Coast. Evergreen forests overlook white sandy beaches cut by rivers and blue lagoons. Antelope, monkeys, and colorful birds live in the forests. And shoals of silvery fish, along with mussels and oysters, live in the clear sea and in the river mouths fringed with mangrove trees.

A hiking trail runs all along The Wild Coast. One of the most beautiful walks is between Coffee Bay and the Hole in the Wall, a huge rock arch standing in the sea.

The Wild Coast and the rolling country inland are the home of the Xhosa people. The Xhosa are traditional cattle herders who count their wealth by the number of cattle they own. They keep sheep and goats for meat and eat beef only on special occasions.

△ **Main Street, King Willam's Town**
The town began as a British army post during the wars with the Xhosa people in the 1830s.

The old Xhosa religion is based on a belief in powerful spirits, such as the Impundulu (Lightning Bird). However, today many Xhosa people are Christians.

East London is a port at the southern end of The Wild Coast. It was built by the British to supply the army headquarters at King William's Town, farther inland. Oxford Street, East London's main street, is named after a street in London, England.

The hero Steve Biko was born in King William's Town. He is also buried here. Biko was a Xhosa who fought against apartheid and died in prison. From King William's Town, a road leads northwest to the city of Alice and Fort Hare University. Nelson Mandela once studied at this famous university for black students. Mandela, who is also a Xhosa, was inaugurated as South Africa's first black president in 1994.

◁ **Xhosa riders in central Transkei** Many Xhosa people wear modern clothes but live in round huts and herd cattle and goats for a living, as they have always done.

△ **Xhosa ceremony** Young men's faces are painted with white clay in the ceremony to mark their entry into manhood. White stands for goodness and light.

THE GARDEN ROUTE

Port Elizabeth is a big, modern city with raised superhighways and car factories. It lies in the south of Eastern Cape Province on the shores of the Indian Ocean and is South Africa's third-largest port. It was here that 5,000 Britons came ashore in 1820 to settle in the country. The town was little more than a stone fort, which still stands today.

From Port Elizabeth, you can visit a nature park that is home to the world's southernmost herd of wild elephants. You may see them drinking from waterholes in the middle of the thornbush scrubland.

Traveling westward along the coast road, you follow the Garden Route, named for its greenery. On the seaward side of the road, Jeffrey's Bay is popular with surfers because of its big rolling waves.

Farther on, large evergreen forests of 1,000-year-old hardwood trees are home to the brightly colored narina trogon bird. The quiet coastal town of Knysna is famous for the hardwood furniture that is made there. An old steam railroad runs between the towns of Knysna and George, passing the lovely Kaaimans River gorge.

▷ **Aloe trees at Dolphin's Point, near the town of George** Surf rolls onto sandy beaches in the bay.

To the north is the high, dry plateau called the Little Karoo and the town of Oudtshoorn. Here, you can visit an ostrich farm and try your skill at the sport of ostrich riding. The local people are expert riders and race against each other. Male ostriches can grow to be nearly 8 feet (2.5 meters) tall.

To the west of George is Mossel Bay. In 1488, Bartolomeu Dias, a Portuguese explorer, dropped anchor in the bay and became the first white person to set foot in southern Africa. The town's museum contains a full-size copy of Dias's ship.

◁ **An ostrich farm at Oudtshoorn** There are many farms like this one around the town. Ostriches are raised for their feathers, meat, and hides. The birds like the hot, dry climate of the Little Karoo.

▷ **Dutch Reformed Church in George** The lovely church was built by Afrikaners in 1842. The ceiling and dome are made of yellowwood and the pulpit of stinkwood. These and other hardwoods grow in the forests nearby.

BEAUTIFUL CITY

Many believe South Africa's loveliest city is Cape Town. The city lies in Western Cape Province at the foot of flat-topped Table Mountain and borders on the Atlantic Ocean. In summer, a refreshing wind, called the Cape Doctor, blows over the city, and the mountaintop is covered in a layer of cloud.

Cape Town is a huge city. It is home to more than two million people and is South Africa's legislative capital. You can visit the fine old Houses of Parliament buildings where South Africa's government meets.

▽ **Cable car going up Table Mountain from Cape Town** It takes five minutes to reach the top. In the background is Lion's Head peak, 2,195 feet (669 meters) above sea level.

△ **Students outside Cape Town University** South Africa's oldest university, built in 1829, stands below Devil's Peak Mountain.

▷ Victoria and Albert Waterfront, Cape Town

Small fishing boats and pleasure craft share the docks in this busy port. Old warehouses have been rebuilt as shops, restaurants, and hotels.

The city of Cape Town was founded by Dutch settlers more than three hundred years ago. They built a stone fortress here called the Castle of Good Hope. It is still used by the South African Army today.

The first African people that the settlers met were the Khoikhoi, who herded cattle. The settlers called them *Hottentots* because of the sound of their language.

Most of Cape Town's people today are of mixed race, part African and part European or Asian. Some are descended from slaves brought here from Malaysia, in the Pacific, to work on the farms. Today Cape Town's Malays are free people. Many of them live in the colorful, flat-roofed houses that line the steep cobblestone streets of the Bo-Kaap quarter. You will also see mosques, where the local people, who are Muslims, come to pray.

From the waterfront, in the north of the city, you can take a boat trip out into Table Bay. Some boats go to Robben Island, which was once a grim prison. Nelson Mandela spent many years here because he opposed apartheid. He was released in 1990.

ON THE CAPE

From Cape Town, a narrow strip of land covered in forest and mountains stretches southward into the Atlantic Ocean. This is the Cape Peninsula. On its western side lies Hout Bay, a busy fishing port. Here you can buy fresh fish from boats at the wharf, or try the famous smoked snoek at one of the town's many restaurants. Some of the fish caught are made into fish oil and fish meal in the town's factories.

On the opposite side of the peninsula is Simonstown, the home of the South African Navy. Martello Tower, which stands in the dockyard, was built by the British as a fort 200 years ago. It is now a naval museum. Downtown, on Main Street, some of the fine old buildings with iron balconies have been turned into shops and cafés. Not far from the town, you can go swimming from a rocky beach shared with a delightful colony of penguins.

South Africa's great wine-growing country begins to the north and east of Cape Town. The vineyards line the hills and mountain valleys and are watered by cool, fast rivers. The first grapes for wine-making were planted by Dutch settlers three hundred years ago. Today, many other fruits, such as peaches and cherries, also grow in the winelands. At the heart of the winelands is the town of Stellenbosch. All around here there are whitewashed houses with tall, curved roof gables. This style of building is called Cape Dutch.

The coast to the southeast of the winelands is famous for whale watching. Between June and November, baby whales and their mothers can be seen playing in the waves at Walker Bay. Farther inland, sheep graze on the slopes of mountains that overlook fields of corn.

▷ **Harvest time in a Stellenbosch vineyard** Grapes for winemaking are picked in February or March. The houses are built in Cape Dutch style.

▷ **Muizenberg, on the Cape Peninsula** Here there are white sandy beaches in a beautiful setting.

▽ **Helderberg Mountains, near Stellenbosch** Footpaths and unpaved narrow roads zigzag up the mountainside.

ACROSS THE WILDERNESS

To the north and west of the winelands is South Africa's main farmland. Here, fields of yellowing corn stretch as far as the eye can see. Farther north, the jagged Cedarberg mountains are the gateway to a vast, beautiful wilderness called the Great Karoo.

"Karoo" comes from an old Khoikhoi word meaning "thirsty land." The sunbaked earth of the Great Karoo can go years with no rain. Only plants such as aloes, which can survive scorching summer days and frosty winter nights, grow here. But wildlife is plentiful, especially in the nature parks. Here you will find curly-horned wildebeests, white rhinos, leopards, and Cape mountain zebras. Herds of springbok roam the dusty plains. The blue crane, the national bird of South Africa, also makes its home here.

The Great Karoo is fringed in the south by thousands of acres of sheep farms and in the northwest by the Namaqualand Desert. After the spring rains, the desert becomes a carpet of yellow, white, and purple flowers before turning brown once again.

Close to Namaqualand's southeastern border with Namibia, the Orange River plunges over a 300-foot (100-meter) ravine. Farther south there are gigantic white sand dunes that make a strange moaning sound when blown by the wind. This wild northern region is called Bushmanland. There are no San, or bushmen, living here now. But you can see the paintings of animals and hunters that they left behind on cave walls at the fringe of the great Kalahari Desert.

To the southeast lies the old mining town of Kimberley. Here, in 1870, two Afrikaner farming brothers named De Beer found diamonds. Later an Englishman, Cecil Rhodes, gained control of diamond mining and developed the company called De Beers.

▽ **The "Big Hole," Kimberley Mine Museum** This is where the De Beer brothers first dug out their diamonds. Later, other prospectors made the hole deeper and wider.

◁ **Giant aloe tree, Goegap Nature Reserve, Namaqualand** The tree is known as the kokerboom or "quiver tree" because San hunters once used its branches to make quivers for their arrows.

▽ **White rhino** Found in many parts of South Africa, white rhino graze the treeless plains for food.

THE BORDERLANDS

Some of the European colonists who left the Cape in the 1830s began a new country in the wilds north of the Orange River. They called their country the Orange Free State and made the small town of Bloemfontein its capital. Now the region is one of South Africa's provinces officially called Free State.

Bloemfontein is a city of skyscrapers and rose gardens. It is also South Africa's judicial capital. This means that the highest judges in the land make decisions here. In the center of the city you will find the earliest of Bloemfontein's four town halls.

It is built of mud brick and has a thatched roof. This is where the government of the old Orange Free State used to meet.

Free State Province borders on the kingdom of Lesotho and the high Maluti Mountains. Some of the little border towns, such as Ficksburg, are very pretty, with sandstone buildings surrounding a town square. Here, in September or October, you can join in Ficksburg's Cherry Festival. Nearby there is a famous weaving center, where Tswana and Sotho women make rugs and sweaters from local wool.

◁ **A luxury swimming pool at Sun City** Two huge vacation resorts—Sun City and Lost City—have been built in the wilds of Northwest Province. They have golf courses, lakes, hotels, and casinos.

▷ **The wild scenery of Free State Province** Yellows and browns are common colors of the *highveld*, the dry grasslands of the South African highlands.

▷ **Children in a hilltop village**
The houses are made of mud and strengthened with wooden beams.

The traditional country of the Tswana people is farther north. Here cattle and sheep graze among the thorn trees on the wide plains. Fields of maize, known as *mealie*, ripen in the sun.

Like the rest of South Africa, the northeastern part is a place for adventure. Here you can see huge 4,000-year-old baobab trees, hike forest trails where there are antelope and leopards, and canoe down rivers that are the home of crocodiles. This is an exciting way to finish your visit to the beautful country of South Africa.

South Africa Facts and Figures

People

Nearly three-quarters of South Africans are black. They include Zulus, Xhosa, Sotho, Tswana, and other peoples. Just over one in eight of the country's population is white. Most whites are Afrikaners, descendants of Dutch settlers. The rest are mainly of English origin. Others include those of mixed race and those who originally came from India.

Trade and Industry

About a third of the world's gold and three-quarters of the the world's platinum are mined in South Africa. Diamonds and other precious stones are also plentiful. Antimony, asbestos, and uranium are among the country's other mineral resources. The sale of minerals to other countries helps to pay for oil, which South Africa has to buy from abroad.

South Africa has huge coal reserves and most power stations use coal. There are also nuclear power stations and hydroelectric dams. South Africa generates about half of all Africa's electricity. Cloth, chemicals, and electronic goods are also important.

△ **Underground in a gold mine** When gold mining began on the Witwatersrand in the 1880s, black people did most of the digging. Still today most mineworkers are black.

Fishing

Huge schools of sardines, herring, and anchovies swim around South Africa's shores. They attract sharks, barracuda, and kingfish. Crayfish, oysters, and other shellfish are also plentiful. Marlin and tuna fish are found where the South Atlantic and Indian Oceans meet. Most fish are caught off the west coast. Deep-sea trawlers take hake, snoek, monkfish, and mackerel from the Atlantic Ocean. South Africa's rivers and lakes have trout, bass, carp, and many other kinds of freshwater fish.

Farming

Less than one eighth of South Africa is farmland. However, the farmers grow enough food to feed the people and to sell food abroad. Corn, wheat, groundnuts, sugarcane, bananas, grapes, cotton, and tobacco are important crops. Wool, from sheep, and mohair, the silky hair of the Angora goat, are other valuable exports. Farmers also raise sheep, pigs, cattle, and chickens. Farm animals are sometimes used to provide leather.

Food

Barbecues, called *braai*, are very popular in South Africa. Grilled meat is often eaten with *mealie* (mashed cornmeal). Fish such as snoek are grilled, fried, or cooked in a spicy sauce. Here are a few other tasty South African dishes:

bredie: mutton cooked with potato and spinach and seasoned with coriander, chili, and rosemary
bobotie: lamb, beef, or venison baked with almonds, apricots, spices, and chutney
biltong: strips of meat dried in the sun until the outside is black but the inside is still red and juicy

28

Schools

Children must complete at least ten years of schooling. Some go to preschool. At five or six, all children enter primary school. They study math, science, a foreign language, and other subjects, including a skill such as woodworking. At the age of eleven or twelve they go to secondary school for up to six years. Some go on to a technical college or university.

The Media

About thirty main daily or weekly newspapers are published in South Africa. Most are in English or Afrikaans. Many other newspapers are published locally, some in African languages. There are around 800 weekly or monthly magazines, covering everything from fashion to sports and politics.

The South African Broadcasting Company (SABC) provides three television channels, including satellite broadcasting. Some of the programs are in English or Afrikaans, others are in African languages. Radio broadcasting includes twenty or so SABC stations in different languages, as well as commercial radio stations.

△ **A giraffe in Kruger Park** Giraffes can grow up to 18 feet (5.5 meters) in height. They live singly or in small herds and feed from trees above the heads of other animals.

Music and Drama

Dance has always been part of the African way of life. Today, South African dance, drama, and music are closely linked. Musical plays often include African dancing, such as the *mapantsula* (township jive), or music such as the *isicataniya* (miners' songs). Some South African classical composers have made use of African drum rhythms and instruments such as the *marimba* (a kind of xylophone). In popular music, styles such as Afro-rock, township jazz and blues, and *kwela* have become famous.

Literature

The first South African poets—the San, Khoikhoi, and Bantu people—told about hunting and nature. Later African poets described the misery of living under white rule.

Afrikaner novelists in the early 1900s often wrote about the struggles of the settlers and the wars with the English. South Africa's most famous novelist, Nadine Gordimer, attacked apartheid. Her best-known book is *Burger's Daughter*. Alan Paton's *Cry the Beloved Country* deals with the tragedy of black people in a society run by whites.

Art

Some of South Africa's rock paintings by the San people are 30,000 years old. They show mainly animals and scenes from the spirit world. Much later San rock paintings are of white settlers with guns. In the 1930s, Helen Vorster made sculptures of the heads of the San, Khoikhoi, and Tswana peoples. Later, new African art began to develop in the townships. Township artists include the painter Louis Maquela and the sculptor Sydney Kumalo.

SOUTH AFRICA FACTS AND FIGURES

△ **A Tsonga woman painting on canvas**
The figures are painted in traditional African style, using bold lines and bright colors. The Tsonga people live mostly near Kruger Park.

Religion

More than three-quarters of South Africans are Christians. The 4,000 or so African Independent Churches are the biggest group, followed by the Dutch Reformed Church. There are also Roman Catholics, Anglicans, and others. About five million follow African traditional religions. Many of South Africa's Indians are Hindus, but some are Muslims and a few are Christians. The Cape Malays are mostly Muslims. Smaller groups include Jews and Buddhists.

Festivals

South Africa has twelve public holidays a year as well as local festivals. Here are a few of them:
 2-3 January **Cape Town New Year Carnival** Big parades draw the crowds into the streets.
27 April **Freedom Day** Celebrates the day when black South Africans first voted
July **Grahamstown Arts Festival** Plays, concerts, films, and art exhibitions are put on.
September-December (dates vary) **Domba Dance** Beer is poured into Lake Fundudzi to honor the Python god of rivers and rain.

Sports

South Africans love the outdoor life and playing and watching sports. Their national cricket and rugby teams, which are among the best in the world, attract huge crowds. So too do soccer, boxing, wrestling, and track and field. Car racing and horseracing also have their fans. Many South Africans enjoy surfing or windsurfing, scuba diving, sailing, and canoeing. Fishing is very popular. Many South Africans also play tennis, squash, and golf. Karate and other martial arts are gaining a following as well.

Plants

Most of South Africa's many different species of plants are heathland plants of the fynbos family. The protea flower is its most famous member. The rain forests have hardwood trees, spiky knobthorn trees, and giant ferns called *cycads*. Flat-topped acacia thorn trees cover parts of the bushveld. Giant fig trees grow in the dry riverbeds, with baobab trees in the far northeast of the country. The deserts support giant aloe trees and the human-looking halfmens tree.

Animals

Elephants, buffalo, lions, leopards, and rhinos (both black and white) are found in game reserves. Leopards also live in the mountain ranges, as do elands, blesbok, zebras, baboons, and the caracal (African lynx). Black wildebeests, springbok, and other animals live on the plains. Reptiles include lizards, venomous snakes such as the Cape cobra and green mamba, and the Nile crocodile. Some birds, such as the green lourie and long-tailed sugarbird, are found only in South Africa.

HISTORY

Early humans lived in southern Africa more than a million years ago. About 30,000 years ago the San people, who were hunters, occupied the region. Later came the Khoikhoi, a cattle-herding people who were descended from the San, and then the Bantu, who worked with iron.

In 1488, the first white people reached southern Africa. These were Portuguese traders who sailed around the Cape on their way to India. Farmers from the Netherlands, who became known as Boers, began to settle in the Cape 200 years later. In the 1800s the British seized the Cape. They fought wars against the Boers as well as the Xhosa, Zulu, and other African people. Many Boers left the Cape to set up new states farther east. There they fought over land with local people. More wars between the British and the Boers followed the discovery of gold and diamonds. The British were victorious, and in 1910 they united the country.

But in the new Union of South Africa, only white people could be elected to government. In 1948 the system called apartheid was introduced, and in 1960 the country cut its ties with Britain.

Under apartheid, nonwhites had few rights. Many opponents of the system were put in prison or killed. But pressure from inside and outside South Africa eventually ended apartheid. Black people voted in government elections for the first time in 1994. They chose former Nobel Peace Prize winner and freedom-fighter Nelson Mandela as the country's first black president.

LANGUAGE

South Africa has eleven official languages. These include English and Afrikaans as well as the languages spoken by black people. For example, the Xhosa and Zulu each have their own language, and the Sotho people have two. Afrikaans developed from the Dutch language of the early settlers. Most white people and people of mixed race in South Africa speak Afrikaans. But English is widely understood across the country. Several other languages are spoken by people of Asian origin.

Useful words and phrases

English	Afrikaans
Zero	nul
One	een
Two	twee
Three	drie
Four	vier
Five	vyf
Six	ses
Seven	sewe
Eight	agt
Nine	nege
Ten	tien
Sunday	Sondag
Monday	Maandag
Tuesday	Dinsdag

Useful words and phrases

English	Afrikaans
Wednesday	Woensdag
Thursday	Donderdag
Friday	Vrydag
Saturday	Saterdag
Good morning	Goeie møre
Good afternoon	Goeie middag
Good night	Goeie nag
Good-bye	Tot siens
Please	Asseblief
Thank you	Dankie
How are you?	Hoe gaan dit met u?
Very well, thank you	Uitstekend, dankie

INDEX

Acknowledgments
Book created for Highlights for Children, Inc. by Bender Richardson White.
Editors: Peter MacDonald and Lionel Bender
Designer: Malcolm Smythe
Art Editor: Ben White
Editorial Assistant: Madeleine Samuel
Picture Researcher: Annabel Ossel
Production: Kim Richardson

Maps produced by Oxford Cartographers, England.
Banknotes from Thomas Cook Currency Services.
Stamps from Stanley Gibbons.

Editorial Consultant: Andrew Gutelle
South Africa Consultant: Jay Heale. Children's Book Specialist, South Africa
Guide to South Africa has been approved by the South African High Commission, London
Managing Editor, Highlights New Products: Margie Hayes Richmond

Picture credits
DKJ = David Keith Jones/Images of Africa. EU/JD = Eye Ubiquitous/James Davis Travel Photography. JvT = Johann van Tonder/Images of Africa. LPL = Link Picture Library. Z= Zefa. t = top, b = bottom, l = left, r = right. Cover: EU/JD. Pages 6-7: EU/JD. 7l: Z. 7r: DKJ. 8: Z. 9t: Lesley Lawson/LPL. 9b: Z. 10: JvT. 11t: Greg English/LPL. 11b: EU/JD. 12-13: Z. 13t: DKJ. 13b: Z. 14: EU/JD. 14-15: EU/JD. 15: EU/JD. 16: Z/Havlicek. 16-17: LPL. 17: Z. 18: DKJ. 19t: DKJ. 19b: DKJ. 20: JvT. 20-21: EU/JD. 21t: Richard du Toit/Images of Africa. 22-23: EU/JD. 23t: Z. 23b: JvT. 24: Orde Eliason/LPL. 25t: JvT. 25b: Z. 26: Hutchison Library/Liba Taylor. 26t: Z. 26b: Z/Boutin. 28: Z/Bramaz. 29: EU/JD. 30: Philip Schedler/Link. Illustration on page 1 by Tom Powers.